The

Importance
of Collecting
Black Art

Naomi Walker-Shields

Dedication

This book is dedicated to my family, extended family and especially to my mom whom I love and miss dearly. Also to the friends who support me in my love of collecting black art.

To Booker Crayton, who like me collects black art and tries to talk me into giving him the pieces that he admires in my collection.

To Antoine Kinard, who encourages me to continue writing. Also, to Frederick Smith and William Stewart Sr. who convinced me to attend college as adult because they thought I would enjoy it and that it would benefit me in my professional career.

To Sharon Braddy, my lifelong friend, who has given me various antiques over our fifty-seven years of friendship. Her husband, Thomas Braddy called it "good garbage."

To my daughters Charmein, Hope and Gina, who laugh when I ask them to give back a painting or piece of art after I do research and decide that I'd rather keep that item. They just laugh and ask what I found out about the artist; then they say no mom you can't have it back.

To my friends Janice W., Jacque M., Dale C., Shirley C., Barbara Finch, Rene L. and Vanessa V., who allow me to rant and rave about art and antiques. Thank you for sharing and understanding.

To Robert 'Words' Taylor, my great- nephew; thanks for encouraging to me. Your new book, 'Wake Up and Start Dreaming," re-ignited my dream.

To the members of the "Writers Group" at the Stony Island Arts Bank for bringing me to the point of publishing my first book. They are all so talented and kind and to Josephine Overby for her editing assistance...couldn't have done it without you. Hugs and kisses to Elisa (Penni) Williams for introducing me to the Writers Group.

A special thanks to my publisher Jo McEntee for all your help in getting this project done.

Thanks to the creator for every blessing!

Acknowledgements

Interviews:

McBride, Mary J. – Sister of artist, William
        McBride, November 28, 1995

Susan V. Polin, LSW, LCPC, Art Therapist
Community Mental Health Council, March,
        1996

Ms. Omar, Professor
September, 1995

Contributors:

Richard Thomas, Poet
Lady with Poem for Backbone, © 1990

William 'Bill' Bonner, Photographer
Photo of the Honorable Harold Washington,
        Mayor of Chicago, IL. 1983-1987

Introduction

I have always loved art. However, I can't paint or draw, not even stick people. I enjoy reading, writing poetry and going to art galleries and museums. My entire adult life has been spent collecting art, specifically Black Art. Do understand that I gravitate toward anything artsy.

While I collect many forms of art, I enjoy the aesthetic effects of visual art. I became interested in art as a result of shopping in resale shops in the 1960s while buying basic home furnishings like sofas, living room chairs and occasional tables for my apartment. I was a young mother with a small budget and an appetite for nice things. Hence, my taste for antique furniture was born. The very first piece I wanted to buy was an old Victrola phonograph. I grew up listening to those old seventy-eight records as my mom and step-father had plenty of them, but they played them on an 'old school' stereo system. Well, I never bought the Victrola because that would have been a luxury item and back then I was in the market for necessities. So my first purchase was an antique ninety inch sofa and a seafoam-green shag rug. From then on, I was hooked...I spent almost all my Saturdays in resale shops all over Chicago and the suburbs. I looked at everything from nick-knacks, jewelry and glassware to paintings, posters and books.

This was also the beginning of my art education.

As I purchased items, I began to learn who made the item, who designed it, who painted it or who manufactured it. Eventually, I began to read articles and books about art. Later on, I realized that an ordinary person like myself, could own art that could be of value one day but most importantly, I learned to only buy the things that I like. Because of that, my personal collection will always be valuable to me. I learned early that you should like the pieces that you buy and choose to live with daily.

My exposure and interest in the arts is ever-growing but my first love is black art. I hope you enjoy my "little book" and that it will open your mind to a whole new world, the world of art. Your choices are unlimited when you think of it.

The Importance of Collecting Black Art

Hello! Hello! Wake up! We're in the twenty-first century and we as a people have made great strides in history...some accomplishments are   acknowledged and well documented and some are not. The most recent feat that we are so proud of was a major success. Our ancestors would not believe it and many people around the world did not think it possible; especially here in the U.S.

Do you have proof of this significant event? Perhaps you have a photograph, a painting, a book, or a song. Maybe a video, a movie, compact disk (CD), a magazine or a newspaper article or perhaps some other new twenty-first century form of media sharing stored in "The Cloud".

Many of us born in the twentieth century are still buzzing and excited about the success and accomplishments of a particular Black man. The whole world was off kilter when it happened. Yes, we the people, elected a Black man to be the President of the United States of America.

I'm addressing this because this is a

really big deal. It was a major accomplishment for a Black man to live in the white house and sit in the oval office as the Commander in Chief of the United States of America. The 2008 presidential election was a historical milestone. Then in 2012 he had the audacity to be reelected, upsetting American politics and Republican politicians from sea to shining sea. To insure that this event is forever in history, we must document, save, and share it. We must preserve our history for future generations. Already the disgruntled politicians are trying to wipe out the "peoples' president's" legacy. Preserving our history is of paramount importance. After all, we want the world to know of our existence and about our culture. The world should also know and remember Barack H. Obama, the forty-fourth President of USA, 2008 – 2016 and Michelle Obama, First Lady of the USA. They were affectionately called POTUS and FLOTUS.

When history is made by a people, it is up to them to tell the story, document the facts, preserve the memory and share the

2

information throughout time. This is so important because it will insure that the history we hold dear is correct in our eyes and not made up by people who know nothing of our struggle, our people or our culture. As you know, so much of black history has been lost, hidden, changed and distorted. Knowing this, we have educated ourselves and can better plan for the preservation and distribution of our own historical facts.

The arts provide an excellent way to preserve and present history. While there are many art forms used to document a culture; literature and visual arts are the most popular forms. Artistic expressions have provided much insight into human society. From the caves of pre-historic times, to today's digital expressions, we enjoy learning about each other.

After my introduction to art, I wanted to own and display art that I liked and would enjoy seeing every day. My early purchases were made at resale shops and estate sales. A small budget and no experience in buying art made these venues my best options at the time. After making a few purchases, I found that I really appreciated art. At this point, I began to research various artists and their works. I learned that some of the art I purchased was actually by known artists and some of my other collectables were of value. It was then that I realized that I preferred Black art. As my interest and knowledge increased, I began to attend auctions, galleries, and museums. I purchased paintings, photos, and books as often as my budget permitted.

The last thirty-five years of collecting have given me a tremendous appreciation for the culture, the art and the history of Black folk. I have met some artists and authors...some famous, some not so famous at the time. I now have personal memories of Margaret Burroughs, William Carter, Marian Howard, George Crump, Gwendolyn Brooks, Toni Cade, Amiri Baraka, Haki Madhubuti and others, including my favorite photographer, William "Bill" Bonner.

In today's world, there are so many

more forms of art due to the development of digital media and computer technology. There is also a new breed of artists. It is now up to the youth and generations to follow, to maintain and to preserve Black history through the arts.

It is my hope that we will continue to collect the art of old and new artists. A list of some modern day artists might include; Betye Saar, Augusta Savage, Annie Lee, Thomas Blackshear, Margaret Burroughs, William Carter, Jean-Michael Basquiat, Elaine Dungill, James Van Der Zee, Brenda Joysmith, William Carter, Marian Howard, Gordon Parks, William Bill Bonner (Bonner & Bonner Photography), Jacob Lawrence, George Crump, Kameelah Janan Rasheed, Jacolby Satterwhite and so many others.

You may not be familiar with some of the people on my list but that's alright. As you know, the art that turns you on depends on your personal taste. When you decide your interests, the fun begins. For me, collecting is both interesting and educational. In my profession as a consultant, I am always learning and art is a history lesson. By looking objectively at a painting or an art object you might think of a time period, of the message you think the artist is portraying or you just might enjoy it for its aesthetic value. Compare it to grown men who collect "Civil War" memorabilia or people who acquire prison art. Once you start getting involved, you might find that your interest may change as you are exposed to more art forms. So please don't let the educational component frighten you, because you don't have to delve into knowing anything about the artist or the piece, if it strikes your fancy. You can purchase what you like, just because you want to own it. There are no rules to collecting what you enjoy. Collecting art is an acquired taste. You get to choose the item, the medium, the subject, the period and many other criteria that please you.

When you become a member of the art world, you also meet new people. You can meet artists, writers, poets, sculptors, patrons of the arts and collectors. You will also find out that some of your friends are also interested in the arts and they will begin to share venues and exhibits that might interest you. The art world is extremely exciting and yet calming to me. I got absorbed in the whole idea of being part of something so beautiful and yet so functional. That is why I do not limit myself to just one form of art. I'm too flighty for that...

In the 60's, I started out collecting old furniture and antique tables; then I incorporated prints and posters. As time flew by, I became interested in oil paintings, lithographs and books. By this time, I understood that I should learn how to enjoy and appreciate art where I find it. Every piece cannot be a "must have" for my collection. I learned very quickly that you shouldn't get so hung up with owning a piece, that you forgo paying a bill to make a purchase. Now don't laugh...you know how it is when you're young and in love, as I was with art, you sometimes do dumb things. Fortunately for me, I learned the ins and outs and some dos and don'ts of collecting. Even though I've been at it for a while, I do not hesitate to say that I'm still growing and learning. I look at almost everything in life as it relates to art. Is it beautiful, is it useful, does it tell a story, does it show feeling and do I want to buy it, save it or sell it or perhaps even give it away? Literature and visual art are most expressive because of how they affect the mind and therefore appeal to different people for different reasons.

Ordinary folk and professional people view and use art differently. For example, the medical community is decidedly involved in the arts. Psychologists often use it to reach patients. Other disciplines use it to design prosthetics or devices to assist their patients, in addition to providing specialized medical care.

In psychology the study of behavior and mental process is the major focus. When you think of it, what better way to study a people, a culture or a society than by examining its art forms? Whether they be paintings, sculptures, drawings, photographs, furniture, architecture, tools, artifacts, video or computer art; they all say something about who we are, what we see, how we think and feel. Art also reflects the artists' preferences and imagination; it can show what we like or dislike, what we do or don't do in daily life and what materials we have available to us. These and many other factors can help to document and understand behavior and or the mental process.

Today, life seems to have so little value and history is being rewritten, both here in the United States and abroad, we as African-Americans must wake up. We must not again miss an opportunity to have input into the chronicling of our history. In the past, this was largely done by others outside of our culture which explains why some parts of our history are incomplete and erroneous. We cannot afford to be deleted from history a second time. We must acknowledge the importance of collecting black art and begin to procure it with quickness.

To emphasize timing, let's start with an interesting article that I read years ago. It was written by Harriet and Harmon Kelley, entitled, "Giving Black Artists Their Due." In this article, Dr. Harmon Kelley, MD and his wife Harriet, tell us how they became interested in collecting black art in 1986, after attending an exhibit at the San Antonio Museum of Art entitled "Hidden Heritage: Afro-American Art, 1800-1950." They launched an all-consuming crusade to learn more about black artists, their struggle and to share this information with others. Per Harriet, "You can take an entire art history class and never hear mention of an African American artist." As a result of this, the Kelley's major focus became obtaining more information and to amass a private collection as soon as possible. In the article, they also addressed the series of events that led to Henry O. Tanner, a famous black artist, leaving the U.S. and moving to Paris in 1891 to escape the racism he found distressing and frustrating. Though Tanner was one of a fortunate few blacks to attend a Fine Arts College, he could not deal with the humiliation and disrespect shown blacks at that time, so he left for Europe.

The Importance of Collecting Black Art

In their drive to win respect for the many forgotten black artists, the Kelleys have demonstrated what an important role the collector can play in the preservation and dissemination of a neglected area of American History and culture. In 1995 one hundred and twenty works of art from the Kelley's collection were organized into an exhibition that toured the country, finishing at the Smithsonian Institute. "It is arguable that African-American art is socially charged, if only because of the odds black artists have had to fight against to achieve success," said the Kelleys. "I think it's important for African-Americans in particular to take pride in the achievements of black artists. It is good to celebrate the struggle of these artists, some of whom went hungry so they could buy art supplies."   "Blacks have long been stereo-typed as lazy, shiftless or dumb and this works hard to negate all those stereo-types. I would also hope it creates some embarrassment that they have not received their just due."

Mary Schmidt Campbell, Executive Director of the Studio Museum in Harlem, says we must not let the artifacts and reminders of our culture get away from us. In an article about collecting black art, she states, "If they get away from us, we'll have no tools with which to teach our children and no evidence of the depths of our cultural identity." Personally, I agree with Ms. Campbell and others like her who passionately collect black art.

You may also be surprised to find that many black artists have strong feelings about their art and their role in society. For example, artist Henry Brownlee believes that the black art of the ghetto should be classified with the 15Th and 16th century masters. On the other hand, Fred Brown, also an artist, believes he has a socio-political responsibility to black people and therefore feels black artists "...cannot remain content with the expression of pure art at the expense of socio-political labors, particularly in the area of subject matter."

Others who might also subscribe to this same school of thought would include a group of young black artists in the post-depression period. Much of their art reflects our way of life at that time. The titles and subject matter depicts sometime subtle and other times blazon messages regarding black life. For example, the painting 'House Rent Party' by Walter W. Ellison, 'Poolroom' by Ramon Gabriel and 'Sunday in the Park' by Archibald Motley, unmistakably document the black experience, and an ethnic cultural undertaking.

It is interesting to note that when I did my research for this project, many of the post-depression artists were still living. Since that time, Margaret Burroughs, William Carter, Annie Lee, William McBride and a few others have died. They were in their 70s and 80s back then, but were still somewhat active in the art community. Much of their art represents a black ethnic cultural undertaking or experience. Annie Lee's art especially speaks to our culture and experience. One look at a few of her paintings will bring back memories of past years or they will make you laugh. Some of them are so whimsical, they will uplift your spirit and cause you to chuckle or bring up a hearty belly laugh.

Mary J. McBride, the sister of artist William McBride states, "They are sometimes referred to as WPA artists." She further explained that this was due to their affiliation with the South Side Community Art Center here in Chicago. The center was one of a hundred neighborhood art centers established under the Depression Era – Works Progress Administration (WPA). Ms. McBride also told me that her brother, William McBride, amassed a collection of works done by "WPA" artists. Some of the works included in his collection are by; Margaret Burroughs, artist, poet and co-founder of the DuSable Museum, George Neal, artist and Joseph Kersey, sculptor. In addition, McBride has the original poster art from the very first Artists and Models Ball in 1941 benefiting the South Side Community Art Center.

Upon realizing my genuine interest in collecting art, specifically black art, Ms. McBride presented me with some excellent press to add to my personal collection. She shared information one never obtains in books written about black artists. Sharing her first hand experiences with me can only be surpassed by actually meeting and talking to some of the "WPA" artists. In fact, I did get a chance to meet William Carter at an art exhibit at the South Shore Cultural Center and Margaret Burroughs at a fundraising art exhibition. I've also visited the South Side Community Art Center many times to view the new exhibits and learn more about the art and artists.

According to an article in the Chicago Sun Times newspaper, the South Side Community Art Center is the only remaining art center established under the WPA Project. The Center continues to sponsor the annual Artists and Models Ball. The Ball is usually held in October. I am fortunate to have invitations to the 1994 and 1995 Balls in my collection. These invitations represent the 55th and 56th year of this celebration of artists and models. They also verify the continued existence of the South Side Community Art Center which received landmark status in 1994.

It is so amazing how an art collection documents a period in time, and a culture or a people. Interestingly enough, an article written by Tonya Bolden Davis, a novice collector, addresses the increased awareness of the value of collecting black art. In the article, she states, "There is also an increasing awareness that black art is in a sense, the American art market's last frontier and as such it is fast becoming a more precious and valuable commodity." Evidence that supports this premise was presented as a result of casual research, due to my own personal interests and pleasures gained from collecting and enjoying certain pieces of art. What I discovered was that increased interest in a period, a particular artist or group of artists, a specific subject matter or medium can affect two things – availability and price.

Works by artists such as Romare Bearden, Varnette Honeywood, Jacob Lawrence and Archibald Motley have increased in price by more than 500%. To personalize the effects of this statement, imagine buying a Romare Bearden collage for $8,000 then six months or a year later a museum curator contacts you and offers you $40,000 for your collage. You now have a serious decision to make regarding the sale of an important piece in your collection. Wow! That's a problem I hope to face one day as a result of the choices I have made in collecting.

While an art collection can add value to an estate or be assimilated as part of an investment portfolio, it is not advisable to go into collecting as a means of reaching financial independence. There are many other important and more rewarding reasons to collect black art. New York businessman Haywood Rogers expressed provocative sentiment when he said, "Our art is a chronicle of how we live, endure and celebrate life; it is the wealth of black people. Hopefully, as more of us become visually literate, we will buy more and spread the wealth."

A few good reasons to start an art collection are; the added enhancement of acquiring a work of art, for the aesthetics and beauty of the piece, for cultural investment, not to mention the preservation of humanities and if it happens to work out that way, as a source of financial investment into the economic status of the black art community. Back in the day I was told that when an artist dies, his or her works become more valuable and sell for a lot of money. Well...I'm not rich yet and I don't know if the paintings or prints have increased in value nor do I know what subject matter is more valuable than another. Because I like my collection, I have not ventured out to find out what is selling or what is of extreme value. I'm not in the market to sell. I tease my children by telling them that I will leave it to them to disperse their inheritance because they're not getting money. At first, they used to tell me to sell, then they started saying give me this one for my home and now my grandson says "Granny I want all of your black art...all of it." It warms my heart to know that my family is now interested in my collection and will continue to save, share and maybe even sell a piece or two in the far away future.

The owner and director of the Evans-Tibbs collection, E. Thurlow Tibbs, believe Black Americans "must promote and finance world appreciation of our culture." What better way to successfully promote "world appreciation" than to assimilate a visual collection of cultural artifacts which document our existence and way of life. A compilation of verbal, written and visual documentation can provide an excellent record for prosperity. We each need to become involved in acquiring parts of our past, current and future heritage.

Sometimes the art collector is an activist, as is the case of Stewart and Lynda Rae Resnick. "We've seen what art can do to create a climate of cooperation and understanding. We've seen what happens when Chicanos and Blacks are able to go to an exhibit that reflects their world and how it helps to unlock that world for others. It is vital as we come to the end of the millennium," says Lynda Rae Resnick. In conjunction with the Los Angeles Museum of Contemporary Art (1995), the Resnicks pledged half a million dollars to create the

Naomi Walker-Shields

VOICE (Venice/Oakwood Inner City
Enterprise), a ceramic factory that produced
collector- edition plates made by former
gang members and unemployed minorities.
The Resnicks, owners of the Franklin Mint
states, "Art is the way we want to serve the
community."

Art in medicine is not new, as I stated
earlier. Social workers and Psychologists
have used artistic expression in the
treatment of certain patients. Have you ever
paid attention to the art in your doctor's
office and various hospital lobbies? Until
recently, I never really gave much thought to
the effects of art in medicine. The following
provides three distinctly different
interpretive uses for art by medical
professionals. Drs. Marc J. Straus and Alvin
Friedman-Kein both attest to the benefits of
art. They both express different types of
medical benefits, professionally and
personally from collecting art.

Dr. Straus states, "In medicine you
have to become a really good observer,
listening closely for subtleties and nuances

that exist from person to person." Art has given me an appreciation for those subtleties..." He explains how he viewed an exhibit by Hannah Wilke, entitled "Intra Venice," and from her photographic exhibit he was able to decipher various medical conditions. He could also determine the extent of suffering and the potential outcome. He returned to the exhibit again and again. Dr. Straus is also a curator. His most recent exhibition is entitled "Inside Out; Psychological Self Portraiture." The show of course includes a self-portrait by Hannah Wilke. "Wilke's photos are metaphorical and spiritual, embodied with the notion that the life/death struggle has its noble and ignoble sides, and we are all vulnerable to the same history, each played out slightly different."

Dr. Friedman-Kien, a dermatologist, on the other hand says, "I think art enriches and nurtures me, not only as a physician but as a person."" What captivates me is that there is a need in every civilization for creating beautiful objects, superb in design and conception." Dr. Friedman-Kien, also said, "I chose dermatology because I'm a very visual person and I chose virology because it can be a very creative field and is on the cutting edge. I'm not sure how my art collecting, which I've done since I was a boy, intersects with my work, but they are intertwined. I'm confronted with mortality every day; living with two thousand or three thousand year old art helps me put it all in perspective." He has found comfort in the timelessness of art, you see. It seems that art in medicine, as in life, expands over many specialties.

While consulting at a mental health center, I was told by various therapists that patient art is sometimes used during sessions to express feeling and past or current situations. Susan V. Polin, LSW, LCPC, an Art Therapist, sometimes uses visual art as a form of therapeutic treatment in the Child and Adolescents' Program. Arts and craft sessions are also a part of the Community Day Treatment Program for adult patients. Some of the art done by patients is really interesting. I have purchased some for my collection.

The Importance of Collecting Black Art

We have seen how art affects the artists, our culture, finances, the economy and the medical community, so let's prepare to assimilate this information and share it with others as we enter the 21st century. Hopefully some of you will give strong consideration to the importance of collecting black art for the preservation of our culture. As we go into the twenty-first century and embark on new experiences, hopefully, we can take under full consideration the responsibility for supporting black artists by serious sponsorship of exhibits and gallery showings. We, on a larger scale, must continue to pool our resources when necessary to ensure that the black art community receives continued support in its efforts to provide us with the tools with which to document our cultural existence and colorful history. After all, if collecting black art is of no interest to us, who will tell our story? Who will tell our story without the effects of black menticide, of "Big Brother", of outside influences, untruths and stereo-types?

Blacks, Hispanics and other

minorities must understand the importance of preserving one's own culture through collecting art and being mindful of the "Black/Hispanic Traditional Psychological Perspective." We must be aware that menticide exists, that we must re-establish our original value system regarding pride and self-respect. We must also become more participatory and vocal in the community. Above all, we should consider, begin and continue to collect Black art for the preservation of a little known, but very important culture in America and world history. We are the only people who can tell our story, as it should be told. After all, it is important to the psychological well-being of our people.

I hope that enough of us will acquire a genuine interest in art, literature or artifacts of our culture so that we can preserve our place in history. To assist you in developing your taste for art, I suggest a visit to a local gallery, neighborhood art center or art museum. Chicago has many such venues all over the city.

The Importance of Collecting Black Art

To get started, "google" black art gallery (include your city if you like). Also, check out these sites; Stony Island Arts Bank, Black Art in America and Diasporal Rhythms. Now you're ready to roll into a new form of entertainment and education. You will learn what excites you and what speaks to your inner being. You will also broaden you circle of friends and acquaintances with the same interests. When I started to attend art functions I met many creative people. At a writers' conference in the 90s I met authors Toni Cade, Gwendolyn Brooks, and Amiri Baraka. Today's artist and authors should be explored and enjoyed. You might have the opportunity to get to know them and their form of art – visual, written or digital. Don't limit your interest. Art is as varied as your interests and imagination. Think about it; you can collect period clothing, computer games, nick knacks (dust catchers), sports and movie memorabilia, books, glassware, porcelain, china, artifacts, toys, gadgets and anything that interests you, including religious icons. Explore, experiment, choose and start collecting.

Naomi Walker-Shields

Support your favorite artists, become a patron of the arts and start buying. Visit some of the art museums and galleries in you city soon.

THE RACE
By Naomi Shields

Thank you God for allowing me to complete
this race
To publish this "little book" before I succumb
to a slower pace
Seems like I had so much fun along the way,
that I'm forced to
Rush to finish my "to do bucket list" come
what may
When you read my book I hope you can say
"I get the message and I'm on my way"
To contribute to our future by remembering
to hold onto
A piece of the past and the present right
now
For a people so strong
A people who are most times treated
despicably wrong
Complete your race but don't do it for me
Do it for the people who are Black, beautiful
and strong
Pick up the mantle and race for success in
doing your part
To document and stress the importance of
completing our

Naomi Walker-Shields

Own private race to create a place in history
For the art of a people that time can't erase

The Importance of Collecting Black Art

I have included photos of some of the art pieces that I collected in the 1980s and 90s. They were taken by me and a friend via camera phones and downloaded into the manuscript. They are not professional pictures...

This project has been a labor of love for me as it was started years ago as a research paper and completed in 1996.
My sincere thanks to old and new friends who encouraged me to develop the paper into a book, thereby, allowing me to accomplish one more thing on my bucket list of personal goals. I have always loved to write, however, most of my writing has been technical or business oriented and sometimes poetry.

I have enjoyed sharing my artistic experiences with you and hope that you embark on your own journey of artistic appreciation.

THE RACE
(A painting by Cortez)

This is oil on canvas mounted on wood, painted August 1998 and given to me as a birthday gift in 2006 by the artist.

The Honorable Harold Washington, Mayor

This is a photo of the first African American Mayor of Chicago Illinois taken by William Bonner, photographer, in the 1980s.

Honey Sweet Sadie
By Marian Howard © 1981

Purchased from, the artist at an art fair in
downtown Chicago, while on lunch. I call her
everybody's grandma.

Harold Washington and William Bonner

The Honorable Harold Washington, Mayor of Chicago Illinois and William Bonner. Harold was the first African American elected mayor of Chicago in 1983. He was elected to two terms, but died in 1987 during his second term.

William 'Bill' Bonner is a Chicago photographer who has photographed many of Chicago's Black elite and ordinary folk. He is a premier portrait photographer. Bill is now retired.

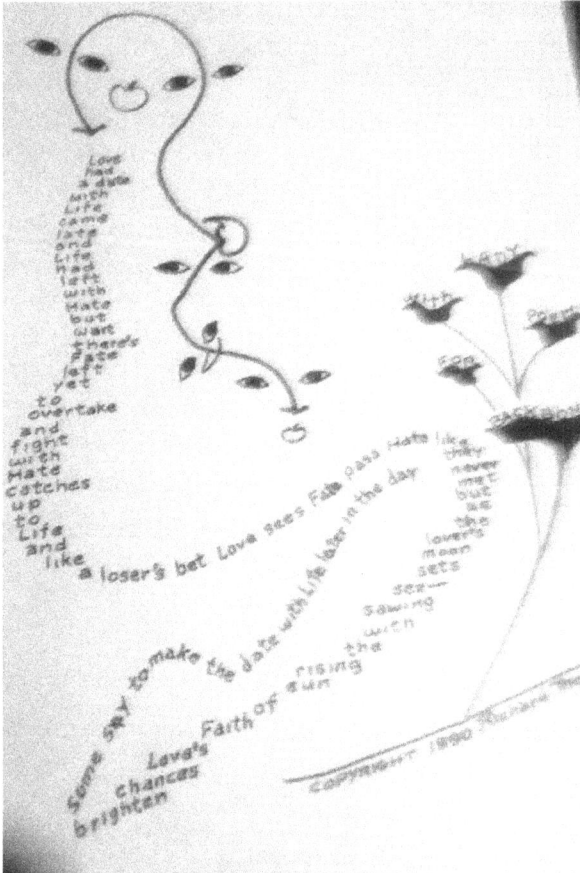

The Lady with Poem for Backbone

This beautiful poem was written by Richard Thomas in 1990. He is a storyteller, puppeteer and humorist. Richard is also a

35

Naomi Walker-Shields

member of the Writers Group at the Stony
Island Arts Bank in Chicago Illinois.

Unique Dolls in My Collection

(1) The 2-headed Pickaninny (one black & one white).
(2) Tiny doll made from safety pins and beads.
 (3) A faceless rag doll in Kente Cloth.
 (4) A faceless Bell Doll.

These are a few of the unique dolls that I've collected over the years in addition to Black designer Barbie, the church doll and Addy, the American Girl Black doll.

Naomi Walker-Shields

Little Books

These little books are a quick read and were purchased in Louisiana when I visited my 105 year old great-aunt in the 1990s.

Three Scoundrels
By
George Crump

George Crump is an accomplished artist
from Chicago. His paintings are bold and
make a definite statement about Black life as
he sees it. Three Scoundrels was painted in
1994. I purchased at one of his private
showings in the 90s.

Naomi Walker-Shields

The Faceless African
By Annie Lee

Annie Lee is famous for her faceless
Paintings. Her first gallery showing was in
1985. Because she sold all of her pieces in
four hours, she allowed prints to be made of
some of her originals.

Doll Play
By
Brenda Joysmith

The lithograph Doll Play was purchased in New Haven Connecticut while visiting my eldest daughter. We visited several antique stores and I found this one and fell in love with it because it reminds me of my three daughters and their cousin when they were growing up. The artist also has Doll Play figurines/collectibles.

Naomi Walker-Shields

I saw this lithograph unframed on ebay
recently for a lot less than I paid for mine.
However, mine came matted and framed so
I'm happy.

The African Princess
By
Elaine Dungill

The African Princess is a lithograph on canvas by Elaine Dungill in 1997. The subject is a direct descendant of an African queen. Dungill is a Chicago native and is also a musician. My lithograph was purchased at an in-home art party given by a friend who

Naomi Walker-Shields

became interested in art for her apartment
when I was selling it part-time.

The Importance of Collecting Black Art

The Tree
By
William Carter

I call this painting the Tree. It has no title or date written on it. It is done in water color on paper and is in its original frame. It is very old. I purchased this painting at a resale store in the 80s and met the artist years later.

Naomi Walker-Shields

Ethnic Print
A Mule Train on a Downgrade

This print is classified as 'Negrobilia". I have
no information on the artist or date of the
painting. This print was also purchased at a
resale shop in the 80s. It is an 'old time
ethnic' piece that I would have never bought
or hung on my wall before I learned to
appreciate black art that depicts our
southern roots.

The Indian Duck Hunter

The photo is a very old (daguerreotype) photograph of an American Indian in a canoe taken around the 1890s.

Bibliographical Entries

Books:

Lewis, Samella S. and Waddy, Ruth G., <u>Black Artists on Art,</u> Los Angeles, Ca. 1969

Chicago Public Library Cultural Center & Chicago Council on Fine Arts, <u>The WPA And The Black Artist,</u> Chicago, New York March 22-April 23, 1978

MAGAZINES & NEWSPAPERS:

Harmon & Harriet Kelley, "Giving Black Artists Their Due" <u>Arts & Antiques Magazine,</u> March 1996 p72

Bolden-Davis, Tonya, "Collecting Black Art" <u>Black Enterprise Magazine,</u> December, 1986 p86-92

"15 Leading Artists" <u>Ebony Magazine,</u> 41:46 May, 1986 (no author given)

Louis, Errol T. "Suppressing Un-Black Art" <u>Essence Magazine,</u> March, 1986, 16:124

Stewart, & Lynda Resnick, "Art Collectors as Activists" <u>Arts & Antiques Magazine,</u> March, 1996 p92

Holg, Garrett, "Recalling A Cultural Oasis on the South Side" <u>Chicago Sun-Times,</u> Sunday, May 9, 1993, Section (B) p9

Marc J. Straus & Alvin Freidman-Kein, "The Healing Art of Collecting," <u>Art & Antiques Magazine,</u> March, 1996 p58

INTERVIEWS:

McBride, Mary J., - Sister of William McBride (WPA Artist)
November, 1995

Susan V. Polin, LCSW, LCPC, Art Therapist
March, 1996

Ms. Omar, Psychology Professor
September, 1995

Naomi Walker-Shields

About the Author

I am a mother, grandmother and a great-grandmother. I am a product of the 1960s. I am a true Chicagoan who loves to travel but can't wait to get back home.

I grew up in the jets on the west side of Chicago in the early 50s. My seven siblings and myself were raised around many different ethnic groups and of course many senior citizens. "It takes a village" was a true statement back then.

I was always a nosey child. My mom said I was that "why (?)" kid...no matter how many questions you answered for me, I would ask why or how come? I wanted to know everything. I loved to talk to my elders because they had lived life and knew a lot of interesting stuff. They knew the history of all things Black, African-American and colored; truth and fable. Sometimes they would repeat the stories, information or tales. But if you get your patience on; you were in for a treat. You can't leave out the younger people either. Mom used to say, "You can learn something from everybody, even a baby". I have been blessed to be introduced to people in their 70s through the 100's.My great-great aunt lived to be 105 years old in Louisiana. Fortunately for me, I visited her before she passed. My adopted God-father (Harry Cecil) lived to be 101years old and died earlier this year. He married Mumsie (Olivia Holley-Cecil) when he was 96 years old. He lived a long and colorful life. He danced right on into glory listening to his favorite tunes...at home with his beloved wife Olivia.

In my life-time I have met and been influenced by many people. Some old, young, rich, poor, educated & uneducated-People of color, white, Hispanic, Indian (American Indian, India and First Nation). In fact, I have lived, worked and commiserated with people of every race, religion (or not), creed and color. Some were good people some were bad and some were crazy as hell but I love them all because they are a valuable part of my life.

Naomi Walker-Shields

The people that have been a part of my life have all taught me something. They have listened to me talk about my greatest concerns of the moment and expressed their thoughts. Communication is the key and for that I thank you.

I have many mantras but my favorites are:

In business: If we don't do business with each other, who will buy our products and service? We must support each other.

Personal: If I can't help you, I sho ain't gonna do nothing to hurt you!

Culturally: If we don't document our culture, life and history; who will? We must tell our own story and history will be closer to the truth.

So I say to you, "Learn about the past, keep up with the present and plan for the future.

The End

www.ingramcontent.com/pod-product-compliance
Lightning Source LLC
Chambersburg PA
CBHW060722030426
42337CB00017B/2973